THE STORY OF THE UNITED STATES

THE POSTWAR ERA:
1945–EARLY 1970S

by Katherine Krieg

WOMEN OF THE WORLD UNITE!

THE PROPOSED E
AMENDMENT

Content Consultant
James Wolfinger, PhD
Associate Dean for Curriculum and Programs
DePaul University

CORE
LIBRARY

Published by ABDO Publishing Company, PO Box 398166, Minneapolis, MN 55439. Copyright © 2014 by Abdo Consulting Group, Inc. International copyrights reserved in all countries. No part of this book may be reproduced in any form without written permission from the publisher. The Core Library™ is a trademark and logo of ABDO Publishing Company.

Printed in the United States of America,
North Mankato, Minnesota
082013
012014

♻ THIS BOOK CONTAINS AT LEAST 10% RECYCLED MATERIALS.

Editor: Mirella Miller
Series Designer: Becky Daum

Library of Congress Control Number: 2013945673

Cataloging-in-Publication Data
Krieg, Katherine.
 The postwar era: 1945-early 1970s / Katherine Krieg.
   p. cm. -- (The story of the United States)
Includes bibliographical references and index.
ISBN 978-1-62403-179-3
1. United States--Civilization--1945- --Juvenile literature. 2. United States--History--1945- --Juvenile literature. 3. United States--Social conditions--1945- --Juvenile literature. 4. United States--Social life and customs--20th century--Juvenile literature.   I. Title.
973.91--dc23
                                                          2013945673

Photo Credits: Anthony Camerano/AP Images, cover, 1; AP Images, 4, 9, 12, 18, 22, 28, 34, 37; U.S. Signal Corps, 7; Red Line Editorial, 11, 21; Bettman/Corbis/AP Images, 15; Image Asset Management Ltd./SuperStock, 24; Gene Herrick/AP Images, 26; Jack Thornell/AP Images, 32, 45; Charles Tasnadi/AP Images, 38

Cover: In the early 1970s, the women's liberation movement gained popularity and support.

CONTENTS

CHAPTER ONE

ECONOMIC BOOM

In the fall of 1945, cities around the United States
held parades in the streets. On August 15, 1945,
World War II (1939–1945) had ended. World
War II was fought among more than 50 countries.
Many world powers had shifted after World War I
(1914–1918). New governments formed, which led
to problems between powerful countries. The United

As World War II ended, many women fought to keep the jobs
they had taken over when the war began.

Women's Roles in the 1950s

Many women stepped up to take industrial jobs that were left open when men went to fight in World War II. But when the war ended and the men returned, most women left their industrial jobs. During the 1950s, it was common for women to stay home and take care of their children and the household while their husbands worked. But as the postwar era went on, many women began pushing for more opportunities outside the home.

States and its allies won World War II. People welcomed soldiers home.

With the end of the war, the United States entered a period of both economic growth and great change. In a few short decades, the country would look very different.

Ending a War

While the end of World War II was a victory for the United States, it left many other countries in bad economic shape. During the war, the United States had allied with the Soviet Union and China. However, the United States worried about these countries' Communist governments. In a Communist country, all

Franklin Roosevelt, right, and the United States'
relationship with Joseph Stalin, left, and the Soviet
Union suffered after the war.

citizens share the country's wealth. The government
owns all properties and businesses. This gives a lot of
power to the government.

The United States feared the Soviet Union and
China would be led by leaders who would try to
take over other countries. Because of this, relations
between the United States and the Soviet Union and
China began to suffer.

Suburban Life

Despite problems with other countries, life in the United States was mostly good. The United States was entering an economic boom.

As young soldiers returned to the United States after the war, they wanted to set up households. To help them, the US government created the GI Bill. This gave 16 million men and women who had served during the war the option to use resources they needed to restart their lives. The GI Bill paid former service members salaries while they looked for jobs. It gave them money for school or job training.

The GI Bill also provided former soldiers with loans to buy houses or start businesses. Because of this, a lot of people bought houses. People began to move outside large cities to neighborhoods called suburbs. As more people moved to these areas, house sales jumped from 142,000 sales in 1944 to more than 1 million sales in 1946.

President Franklin D. Roosevelt signed the GI Bill in 1944 to help soldiers restart their lives.

Many people started new companies too. Some companies became large corporations. A corporation is a group of employers and employees organized as a group. People started to take jobs providing services instead of making things. Many Americans considered themselves part of the middle class. That meant they lived comfortably. They could afford their basic needs, plus they had extra money for shopping and activities.

The Rise of Television

In the late 1940s, television was a brand-new technology for most Americans. Televisions became more popular after the war. Sales increased by 500 percent as more Americans bought televisions. The number of television stations increased from nine to 48 between 1945 and 1948.

But other Americans still struggled. Small family farms, for example, could not compete with large farming corporations.

Pushing for Change

After the war, many Americans also began to think about how they could improve their country. At this time, African Americans did not have the same rights as white Americans. For example, African-American children and white children had to go to separate schools. The schools for African Americans were often in poor shape. This separation, known as segregation, was the law in the South. It was not always followed in the North.

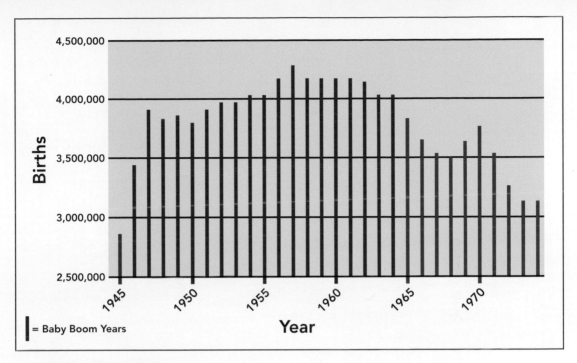

Births

4,500,000

4,000,000

3,500,000

3,000,000

2,500,000

1945   1950   1955   1960   1965   1970

Year

| = Baby Boom Years

Baby Boomers

From the late 1940s to the mid-1960s, many Americans had children. This was called the baby boom. The chart below shows the number of US births during this time. What does the chart tell you? How does this chart connect to what you have learned in Chapter One?

On May 17, 1954, things changed. The court case *Brown v. Board of Education* ended with the decision that US public schools had to allow all children to attend the same schools—no matter their race. This was an early step toward racial equality in the United States. But it was only the beginning of a long struggle.

CHAPTER TWO

THE THREAT OF COMMUNISM

The United States became serious about keeping Communism from spreading to other countries during the postwar era. Meanwhile many Communist governments worked to gain more land. This led the United States into more conflicts and wars.

As Communist governments expanded, the United States sent troops overseas for possible action.

The Korean War

With World War II still in recent memory, the United States soon entered the Korean War (1950–1953). North Korea and South Korea split after World War II. On June 25, 1950, Communist North Korea invaded South Korea. Worried the fall of South Korea would cause Communism to spread throughout Asia, the United States decided to help South Korea.

US forces entered South Korea on June 30, 1950. The United Nations also sent troops to South Korea on September 15. By the end of 1950, China was bringing in troops to help North Korea.

After more than two years, the war finally ended on July 27, 1953. No land had been gained for either side. The border between the two countries remained the same as before the war.

The Cold War

While the United States was fighting in Korea, they were involved in the Cold War too. The Cold War was not an actual war. It was a period of tension between

The United States and the Soviet Union worried the other country would attack with a dangerous atomic bomb.

the United States and the Soviet Union that lasted from 1947 to 1991.

Both countries had powerful nuclear weapons. These weapons were very destructive. Many people believed a major nuclear war was around the corner.

NASA

The United States wanted to learn more about outer space. It created the National Aeronautics and Space Administration (NASA) on October 1, 1958. NASA would focus on space exploration and technology.

Some people built bomb shelters in their basements or backyards to protect themselves if this happened. Both countries kept a close eye on each other.

The Space Race

The United States and the Soviet Union also competed to have the best technology. Whichever country had the best technology could make the best weapons. On October 4, 1957, the Soviet Union launched the first satellite to successfully orbit Earth. The satellite's name was Sputnik I.

Many Americans were concerned about Sputnik. If the Soviet Union could send a satellite into space, they could launch missiles carrying nuclear weapons to the United States. The two countries competed to improve their knowledge of outer space. This was called the "space race."

Meanwhile Communism spread to other countries. The United States tried to prevent Communism from taking over a country whenever it could. This would lead the United States into one of its longest wars yet.

FURTHER EVIDENCE

There is a lot of information about Communism and how the United States reacted to it in Chapter Two. One example given is the Korean War. What is the main point of the chapter? What evidence was given to support that point? Visit the Web site below to learn more about the Korean War. Choose a quote from the Web site that relates to this chapter. Does the quote support the author's point about the Korean War? Write a few sentences explaining how the quote you found relates to this chapter.

The Korean War
www.mycorelibrary.com/postwar-era

CHAPTER THREE

WAR AGAIN

The United States became involved in yet another war in 1955. Again it involved a Communist nation. This time the war was in Vietnam. Like Korea, Vietnam had been divided into two countries. A Communist government ruled North Vietnam but not South Vietnam. North Vietnam was trying to unite the whole country under the Communist government.

South Vietnamese troops get ready for war against North Vietnam. The United States came to South Vietnam's aid in 1955.

A New Kind of War

The Vietnam War was different from the other wars the United States had been involved in. The North Vietnamese used a battle tactic called guerrilla warfare. In previous wars, soldiers marched across battlefields and took cover in dirt trenches. Guerrilla soldiers hid in the bushes and fired at their targets. They set booby traps and traveled in underground tunnels. US military commanders in Vietnam had difficulty adjusting to this new kind of war.

The United States worried that if all of Vietnam became Communist, Communism would spread throughout Asia. The United States decided to help South Vietnam fight North Vietnam. In 1955 they sent in supplies to help. In 1961 the United States sent soldiers to fight too. By 1962 there were 9,000 US troops fighting for South Vietnam.

Many people in the United States expected the war in Vietnam to be won quickly. But it was more difficult than they thought. As the war dragged on, some people began to question

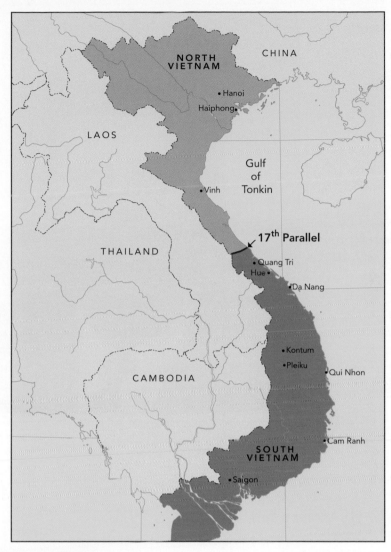

Divided Vietnam

Vietnam was divided at the 17° latitude line. The division was known as the 17th parallel. This map shows the division of Vietnam. After reading about the Vietnam War, how does the map help you to understand the conflict? Is it different than you expected? What have you learned about the Vietnam War from looking at this map?

Newly elected president John F. Kennedy wanted to see the United States make progress during his term, but it would be a challenge.

whether the Vietnam War was a good idea in the first place. US troops left Vietnam in 1973.

The Cuban Missile Crisis

John F. Kennedy was elected as president of the United States in 1960. He replaced President Dwight D. Eisenhower. Kennedy was a popular president. He promised progress for the American people.

But, like all the presidents of this era, he faced some big challenges.

In addition to the Vietnam War, the United States was still in the midst of the Cold War. They were concerned about partnerships between Communist countries such as the Soviet Union and Cuba.

In October 1962, a US spy plane flying over Cuba took pictures of Soviet nuclear missiles stationed on the island country. Because Cuba is close to the United States, people believed the missiles could reach US shores if they were launched. This greatly worried US officials, including Kennedy.

President Kennedy

President Kennedy was one of the most famous people of the 1960s. He became the thirty-fifth president of the United States in 1960. At age 43, he was one of the youngest presidents ever to take office. He was also the first Roman Catholic president. Kennedy's presidential term and life were cut short when he was assassinated on November 22, 1963, in Dallas, Texas. The nation mourned its leader.

Missile Ready Tent

Fuel Trailers

Former Launch Positions

Former Location of Missile-Ready Tents

This aerial photo shows a missile launch site in Cuba. President Kennedy later sent ships to investigate.

Kennedy sent navy ships to circle the island of Cuba. The ships would attack if Cuba launched the weapons. Kennedy told Soviet Union leader Nikita Khrushchev he would not move the ships until the weapons were moved and facilities in Cuba were destroyed.

The United States and the Soviet Union were on the brink of nuclear war. After several tense days, Khrushchev agreed to Kennedy's demands. But he also required the United States to remove its own nuclear missiles from Turkey, which was near the Soviet Union.

Nuclear war was prevented for the time being. But the United States would face more challenges in the next decade.

EXPLORE ONLINE

The focus in Chapter Three was on the Vietnam War. The Web site below focuses on the Vietnam War too. As you know, every source is different. How is the information on the Web site different from the information in this chapter? What information is the same? How do the two sources present information differently? What can you learn from this Web site?

Vietnam Online
www.mycorelibrary.com/postwar-era

CHAPTER FOUR

EQUAL RIGHTS

Things were changing in the United States, and people noticed. People started to believe change was something that could happen soon. At this time, many people were treated unjustly simply because of the color of their skin.

In many southern states, Jim Crow laws kept African Americans and white people segregated. This meant they were kept apart because of their race.

Peaceful protests, like that of Rosa Parks' bus protest, became more frequent in the 1960s.

Jim Crow laws separated African Americans from white people. Bathrooms, waiting rooms, and buses were just a few places that were segregated in the South.

The Jim Crow laws were racist rules that were meant to keep African Americans and other people of color from having the same rights as white people.

African Americans were not allowed to use the same bathrooms or drinking fountains as whites. They were not allowed to sit at the front of the bus and had to stand if there was not enough room for everyone to sit. White people and African Americans were not allowed to marry one another.

African Americans were also often passed over for jobs in favor of white people. Sometimes people with racist views hurt or murdered African Americans.

Leaders for Rights

African Americans had been working toward more rights for decades. The civil rights movement grew in the 1960s. African-American leader Martin Luther King Jr. had helped run the Montgomery Bus Boycott that started in 1955. African Americans stopped riding buses in Montgomery, Alabama, until the city government changed the segregation law on buses. King was seen as the leader of the civil rights movement after this boycott. He helped run peaceful protests around the country. He hoped to draw attention to the mistreatment of African Americans.

The Black Power Movement

Not everyone believed in King's nonviolent approach. Some African Americans felt they would have to separate themselves from white people to have equality. They wanted African Americans to have an entirely separate culture from whites. These ideas became part of the black power movement. A man named Malcolm X helped lead this movement. Some people in the movement wanted to use force to get equality. But the civil rights movement and King's nonviolent approach eventually proved more popular.

A Hopeful Future

Things began to improve little by little. But it was not without hard work. African Americans and their allies staged countless boycotts, sit-ins, and other peaceful protests. They often risked their lives to bring attention to injustice. In 1963 King led people in a march in Washington, DC. More than 200,000 people attended.

In June 1964, the Civil Rights Act of 1964 was passed. This act ended Jim Crow laws. It also ended religious discrimination and discrimination against women. African Americans celebrated their victory. But many people in the South were angry about the change. Sometimes they acted with violence that ended in arrests or death. King and his followers continued to push for equal rights despite the dangers.

On April 4, 1968, King was assassinated in Memphis, Tennessee. His followers pressed on without him. The Civil Rights Act of 1968 was passed in April. This made it illegal to keep people from buying or renting housing based on their skin color.

Civil Disobedience

King and his followers used a technique called civil disobedience to gain attention for their cause and to push for change. They held peaceful demonstrations where they broke laws they believed were unfair. Some African Americans used areas that were supposed to be only for white people. They would allow themselves to get arrested for breaking these laws. Civil disobedience was a way to peacefully point out that the laws were wrong. One example of civil disobedience was called a sit-in. This is a form of protest in which people occupy an area until their demands are met.

Martin Luther King Jr. leads a peaceful protest march through the streets of Memphis, Tennessee.

The civil rights movement inspired other groups to stand up for their rights too. As the 1960s came to a close, there was still a lot of work to be done. African Americans had full equal rights but were still not treated equally.

Martin Luther King Jr. gave his famous "I Have a Dream" speech at a 1963 march in Washington, DC. The following is an excerpt from the speech:

> I say to you today, my friends, so even though we face the difficulties of today and tomorrow, I still have a dream. It is a dream deeply rooted in the American dream.
>
> I have a dream that one day this nation will rise up and live out the true meaning of its creed: "We hold these truths to be self-evident: that all men are created equal." . . .
>
> I have a dream that my four little children will one day live in a nation where they will not be judged by the color of their skin but by the content of their character.
>
> I have a dream today.
>
> Source: "I Have a Dream Speech (TEXT)." Huffington Post. TheHuffingtonPost.com, January 17, 2011. Web. Accessed May 13, 2013.

What's the Big Idea?

Take a close look at King's words. What is his main idea? What evidence is used to support his point? Come up with a few sentences showing how King uses two or three pieces of evidence to support his main point.

CHAPTER FIVE

AN ERA OF CHANGE

The civil rights movement led many people to think more seriously about human rights. Many other groups began fighting for equality. Women began to question their roles in US society.

The Women's Liberation Movement

Women had fewer job opportunities than men in this era. The Civil Rights Act of 1964 was supposed to make sure all people were paid equally. But many

Betty Friedan was a leader of the women's liberation movement who demanded equality for men and women.

businesses still paid women less than men. It was difficult for women to support themselves. Women depended on their husbands for money. Unmarried women often struggled to provide for themselves and their families.

These concerns led to the women's liberation, or feminist, movement in the early 1970s. Some women protested and held marches to bring attention to their cause. Many worked to pass laws to give women equal opportunities. Some people worried working women would not be able to care for their families.

Hippies

In the 1960s and 1970s, some Americans decided to live a different lifestyle. They were called hippies. Hippies stayed away from the mainstream middle-class society. Many of them were young people, and most hippies did not believe in war. Some hippies held protests or sit-ins to pressure the government to end the Vietnam War.

Wars End and Continue

The Vietnam War continued through the 1960s. People became more and more unhappy

All US troops left Vietnam by early 1973, but the war did not end until two years later.

about the war and held antiwar protests. Efforts to leave Vietnam began in early 1972. All US troops left Vietnam on March 29, 1973.

The United States ended its involvement in Vietnam, but Communism continued to spread around the world. The Cold War continued until the early 1990s.

Trouble at Home

The United States also faced problems within its borders. Most Americans believed their elected

The Watergate scandal during Nixon's presidency eventually caused him to retire from office. The scandal made many Americans uneasy about their government.

leaders were trustworthy. But in the early 1970s, Americans discovered their president had lied to them.

On June 17, 1972, burglars were caught stealing important documents from the office of the Democratic National Committee. The office was located in the Watergate building in Washington, DC.

By August 1974, it was revealed the president at the time, Richard Nixon, allowed this to happen. Although Nixon tried to cover up that he knew about the burglary, he eventually resigned. Nixon is the only president to resign from office. This scandal became known as "Watergate." Watergate made some Americans wonder if they could trust their leadership.

The First Internet Connection

The first Internet connection was called the Advanced Research Projects Agency Network (ARPANET). The first Internet communication happened in October 1969. Messages were sent through ARPANET from computers at the University of California at Los Angeles to computers at Stanford Research Institute in Stanford, California. At this time, people thought the Internet could be a useful tool for the US military.

Changes in Technology

As the postwar era ended, there were changes in technology. These changes would shape the country's future. The US military began to develop the Internet in the 1960s. The first e-mail service was created in 1976. It was called Comet. The digital age was about to dawn and bring the country into a new era.

The postwar era was a time of great change in the United States. When the era ended, many people in the United States had gained new rights. But the United States had also lost alliances with many countries. As Americans looked forward, the next era promised many new opportunities and challenges. How would technology advance? Would Communism continue its spread around the world? Americans anxiously waited to see what would happen next.

Betty Friedan, a leader in the women's liberation movement, wrote a book titled *The Feminine Mystique*. It was first published in 1963. Friedan's book discusses the roles of women during the postwar era:

> *The problem lay buried, unspoken, for many years in the minds of American women. It was a strange stirring, a sense of dissatisfaction, a yearning that women suffered in the middle of the twentieth century in the United States. Each suburban wife struggled with it alone. As she made the beds, shopped for groceries, matched slipcover material, ate peanut butter sandwiches with her children, chauffeured Cub Scouts and Brownies, lay beside her husband at night, she was afraid to ask even of herself the silent question: "Is this all?"*
>
> Source: Betty Friedan. The Feminine Mystique. New York: Norton, 2001. Print. 57.

Changing Minds

Friedan gives her viewpoint on women's roles during this era. Take a position on women's roles in the postwar era. Imagine your best friend has the opposite opinion. Write a short essay trying to change your friend's mind. Make sure you state your opinion and your reasons for it. Include facts and details that support your reasons.

IMPORTANT DATES

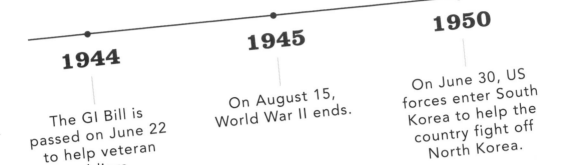

1944

The GI Bill is passed on June 22 to help veteran soldiers.

1945

On August 15, World War II ends.

1950

On June 30, US forces enter South Korea to help the country fight off North Korea.

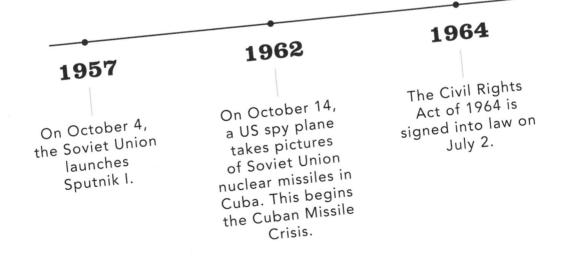

1957

On October 4, the Soviet Union launches Sputnik I.

1962

On October 14, a US spy plane takes pictures of Soviet Union nuclear missiles in Cuba. This begins the Cuban Missile Crisis.

1964

The Civil Rights Act of 1964 is signed into law on July 2.

1953

1954

1955

On July 27, the Korean War ends.

All US schools are integrated after the May 17 verdict for Brown v. Board of Education.

The Vietnam War begins on November 1.

1968

1973

1974

The Civil Rights Act of 1968 is passed on April 11.

On March 29, all US troops leave Vietnam.

On August 9, Nixon resigns from office because of the Watergate scandal.

Tell the Tale

Chapter Four discusses Jim Crow laws that kept African American and white people separated. Write 200 words that tell the story of someone who was affected by these laws. How did that person feel? What should he or she have done? Be sure to set the scene, develop a sequence of events, and offer a conclusion.

You Are There

Chapter Two discusses some of the fears people had about the Cold War. The Cuban Missile Crisis was an especially scary time for many Americans. Imagine you are a boy or girl living in the United States when the Cuban Missile Crisis occurs. Knowing your country could be on the brink of nuclear war, how do you feel? What steps will you and your family take to make sure you are safe?

Why Do I Care?

This book discusses the civil rights movement that happened more than 50 years ago. But people still talk about it today. Even though you did not experience the movement, how does it connect to your life? Write down two or three ways the civil rights movement connects to your life.

Say What?

This era of US history presents a lot of new vocabulary. Find five words in this book that you've never heard before. Use a dictionary to find what they mean. Then write the meanings in your own words. Use each word in a new sentence.

GLOSSARY

allies
partnerships between two or more people, groups, or countries with shared goals

assassinate
to murder a well-known person, usually for a political reason

boycott
to attempt to change something by not purchasing certain items or using certain services

feminine
a characteristic of being female or being womanly

injustice
something that is unfair or wrong

orbit
to circle around something

satellite
a device that circles Earth from outer space and sends back messages

scandal
a shameful or dishonorable event

sit-in
a form of protest in which people occupy an area until their demands are met

suburb
towns that are next to large cities

LEARN MORE

Books

Callan, Jim. *America in the 1960s.* New York: Facts On File, 2005.

Hall, M. C. *Martin Luther King Jr.: Civil Rights Leader.* Edina, MN: ABDO, 2009.

Perritano, John. *Vietnam War.* New York: Scholastic, 2010.

Web Links

To learn more about the postwar era, visit ABDO Publishing Company online at **www.abdopublishing.com**. Web sites about the postwar era are featured on our Book Links page. These links are routinely monitored and updated to provide the most current information available. Visit **www.mycorelibrary.com** for free additional tools for teachers and students.

INDEX

ABOUT THE AUTHOR

Katherine Krieg is an author and editor of many books for young people. She is currently working toward a master of fine arts in writing.